TAROT
for the
BEGINNER

A Simple & Easy
Step-by-Step Guide
to Reading the Tarot Cards
in One Hour or Less!

PSYCHIC DAYLE SCHEAR

GW00570756

Blue Dolphin Publishing, Inc.
1994

Also by Dayle Schear

Dare to Be Different!
The Psychic Within: True Psychic Stories
Tarot for the Beginner (video)
What If? (forthcoming)

Copyright © 1994 Dayle Schear
All rights reserved.

Published by Blue Dolphin Publishing, Inc.
P.O. Box 1920, Nevada City, CA 95959
Orders: 1-800-643-0765

ISBN: 0-931892-92-9

  Library of Congress Cataloging-in-Publication Data
Schear, Dayle
    Tarot for the beginner : a simple & easy step-by-
  step guide to reading the tarot cards in one hour or less
  / Dayle Schear.
        p.   cm.
    ISBN 0-931892-92-9 : $6.95
    1. Tarot.   I. Title.
  BF1879.T2S34 1994
  133.3'2424—dc20   94-10402
                                        CIP

Illustrations from the Rider-Waite Tarot Deck repro-
duced by permission of U.S. Games Systems, Inc., Stam-
ford, CT 06902 USA. Copyright © 1971 by U.S. Games
Systems, Inc. Further reproduction prohibited. The
Rider-Waite Tarot Deck is a Registered Trademark of
U.S. Games Systems, Inc.

Printed in the United States of America by
Blue Dolphin Press, Inc., Grass Valley, California

10   9   8   7   6   5   4   3   2   1

TABLE OF
CONTENTS

Good Luck! Have Fun!

This is a step-by-step guided book to teach you how to read the Tarot cards.

This Tarot guide is an easy method to use. If you follow the easy steps, you will be reading the cards in as little as one hour.

TAROT
FOR THE
BEGINNER

TAROT INSTRUCTIONS

How to Read the Cards and Lay Them Out

1. Preferably use the Rider-Waite Tarot Deck, which can be purchased at most bookstores, or any metaphysical bookshop.

2. Freshly open the new deck of Tarot cards, put aside the box, and glance through the cards. There should be two cards that do not belong in the deck—they are white with print on them; please put these cards to the side, as they will not be used.

3. Shuffle the cards in rhythm. Do not cut the deck in half and shuffle. Keep shuffling for at least five minutes. The reason for this is that you are putting your energy into the cards, and they are becoming part of you.

4. Spread the cards on the floor face down and mix the cards thoroughly for about five minutes or so, turning them in every direction.

5. Make sure some of the cards are reversed. This is the only time you will reverse the cards. When you glance through the whole deck,

1

some cards will be reversed and some cards will be upright. This way they will be thoroughly mixed.

6. Now pick up the deck and shuffle without breaking the rhythm, or the shuffle.

7. Ask the cards a specific question as you are shuffling, for example, "Will my business improve?" "Is John the one I should marry?"

8. Sometimes the cards will not answer your question. The cards will tell you what you need to know instead; so don't be discouraged.

9. When your gut feeling inside tells you to stop, put the cards down toward the left side of you, and let them rest.

Now, let's pick a court card for you!

COURT CARDS

Let's pick a court card. A court card represents you, or someone for whom you are reading. If you are reading for yourself, pick a court card that best describes yourself. Remember, a court card represents a person. If you are reading for your client or friend, pick a court card that best describes your client.

Court Card Description

Emperor	Not a court card but can be used as one; represents a man of power.
Empress	Not a court card but can be used as one; represents a woman of power.
King of Wands	Use this card for a businessman.
Queen of Wands	Use this card for a businesswoman.
Page of Wands	A young girl or boy who brings joy into your life.
Knight of Wands	A man who likes to create change.
King of Cups	Father-type image; husband, good and kind.

<u>Queen of Cups</u>	Mother-type image; good woman.
<u>Knight of Cups</u>	Young girl, boy or child, a romantic dreamer.
<u>Page of Cups</u>	Girl or boy, can represent a homo-sexual.
<u>King of Swords</u>	A lawyer or govern-ment official.
<u>Queen of Swords</u>	A widow or divorced person.
<u>Knight of Swords</u>	A romantic suitor; one who is courting you.
<u>Page of Swords</u>	Young person, boy or girl, who has a big mouth and spies on you, or others, and tells all.
<u>King of Pentacles</u>	Use this card for a wealthy man.
<u>Queen of Pentacles</u>	Use this card for a wealthy woman.
<u>Knight of Pentacles</u>	Use this card for a young person who does his work well.

| Page of Pentacles | Use this card for a young child (boy or girl), one who studies as a scholar, or a child going to school. |

Wands	Represents all business matters.
Cups	Represents all matters of love.
Swords	Represents sorrow and illness.
Pentacles	Represents all money matters.

Now that you have chosen your court card, place the court card
           In Front of You on the Table.

Shuffle the rest of the deck until your gut feeling tells you to stop. Please do not stop shuffling till you get that feeling. Always have a specific question in mind while shuffling.

Now stop shuffling, and put all the cards down toward your left, except for your court card, the one which you have picked out earlier. This card should now be facing you on the table. Please look at the layout on the next page.

Tarot Card Layout

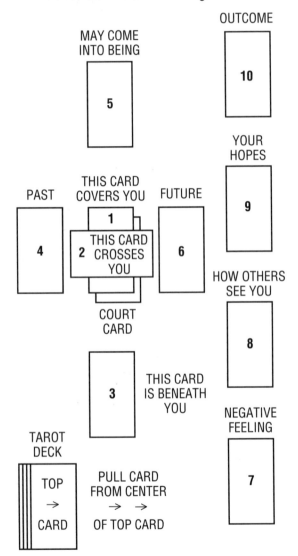

OUTCOME
10

MAY COME
INTO BEING
5

YOUR
HOPES
9

THIS CARD
COVERS YOU

PAST
4

FUTURE

1

THIS CARD
2 CROSSES
YOU

6

HOW OTHERS
SEE YOU
8

COURT
CARD

THIS CARD
IS BENEATH
YOU

3

NEGATIVE
FEELING
7

TAROT
DECK

TOP
→
CARD

PULL CARD
FROM CENTER
→ →
OF TOP CARD

THE LAYOUT

<u>Court card</u>	<u>This is you, your court card, the one on the table.</u>
Card 1	This card covers your court card; <u>always read upright.</u>
Card 2	This card crosses you and represents that of crossing you for good or bad; the card <u>is read upright.</u>
Card 3	This card is beneath you and concerns your problem.
Card 4	This is the past, that which is on the way out.
Card 5	This is what crowns you and may come into being.
Card 6	This is your future, concerning your question.
Card 7	This is your own negative feelings about the problem.
Card 8	This is how others see you.
Card 9	This card represents your hopes.
Card 10	This card is your outcome.

Read all the cards together to form the conclusion to your question.

There is more than one way to lay out the cards. I am teaching you the Celtic Cross method. I have found this method to be the easiest to work with. Since this book is being written for the beginner, I would prefer you to stick with this easy, simple method.

However, if you wish to know deeper meanings of the cards, or you wish to have your question answered to the fullest, you may lay the cards out again and go around two more times for deeper meaning. This means you may lay the cards out three times by following the Celtic Cross method. But don't go around more than three times.

Here is a hint to remember: While shuffling the cards just before you do the layout, if *a card accidentally falls* out of the deck, this card is trying to tell you something; read that card before you do your layout and take *special meaning* of that card. If that card should fall into your spread, note the position of the card and take *special meaning* of what the card is trying to tell you.

Another tip: If the same cards come up over and over again in a layout, even if you have asked a different question, take special note: the cards are trying to tell you something. They may be telling you something you don't want to hear. Listen! Sometimes the cards foretell what is going to happen. At other times the cards answer your question.

MAJOR ARCANA CARDS

0. The Fool
1. The Magician
2. The High Priestess
3. The Empress
4. The Emperor
5. The Hierophant or Pope
6. The Lovers
7. The Chariot
8. Strength
9. The Hermit
10. Wheel of Fortune
11. Justice
12. The Hanged Man
13. Death
14. Temperance
15. The Devil
16. The Tower
17. The Star
18. The Moon
19. The Sun
20. Judgment
21. The World

0
The Fool

Meaning: Think twice before you rush head-on into any situation. Choices are ahead of you. The fool always means there is a "choice"; you will be at the crossroads of a major decision. Think carefully as you travel along your path; there is more than one option: whether to remain a fool, or go on to great heights, is up to you. This can also be a person going into a new venture, a new job or relationship. Think twice, or you may become a "fool."

The Fool Reversed

When the Fool is reversed, there is a warning that you will be making a faulty decision. A wrong choice is coming your way—think twice, or you will end up looking like a fool.

I
The Magician

Meaning: Skill with business matters. This can mean the start of a new business or a new enterprise. New skills being used: you are able to use your education in a new business venture, original ideas, with seeds of growth. This can also mean new arts and crafts, or imports and exports. This card will always appear before a brand new business venture.

The Magician Reversed

Time is not right to venture into any new business deals. There may be trickery and fraud; look carefully before you hand over any money in any new business venture. If you are being asked to join a new company, think twice: you may not like the people with whom you will be working.

II
The High Priestess

Meaning: There are hidden meanings in the cards; the cards will not tell all. This is the beginning of psychic abilities, and the highest state of intuition. This card is teaching you to go ahead with psychic studies. If you are look-ing for a teacher to help you, one will come. In a love situation, you are not in possession of all the facts; more of the facts should be revealed to you soon. Just wait.

The High Priestess Reversed

Nothing is hidden to you; everything is being laid out. Don't trust just anyone at this time. You must analyze the situation thoroughly in business or in a love situation. If you are in a love situation and not getting the support you need, ask your lover for a deeper commitment.

III
The Empress

Meaning: The card of fertility and growth. She can be used as a court card. Card of abundance; can mean a child on its way, card of a birth in the family. In a man's reading, this woman represents a warm and loving woman who makes him feel wonderful. If one is thinking of getting married, this will be a good marriage; or if one is moving to a new place, this will be a good move.

The Empress Reversed

Just a little bit of self-indulgence, overdoing it. Also indicates infertility, probably temporary, or an unwanted pregnancy. See how it fits in your life.

IV
The Emperor

Meaning: The boss, a man of power, a leader. Can be used as a court card. When this person enters into your life, you will not be able to ignore him; he may be a boss, a political leader, or a very strong husband who is extremely skillful and clever. If you are asking about a man and this card shows up, he is all that he appears to be. He can take charge in any given situation.

The Emperor Reversed

Don't trust this man; he may appear to be very strong, but is unstable. He may have alcoholic or drug tendencies.

THE HIEROPHANT

V
The
Hierophant
or Pope

Meaning: One who conforms to work or any given situation. Usually this represents a situation that you will have to face, in business or work. You will have to conform, whether you like it or not. If this represents a person who is in your life, this person is very conservative. It may be a teacher, a priest, your boyfriend, or husband—whomever it is, he conforms. This person believes in tradition, and he offers advice that will help you in the near future.

The Hierophant Reversed

You can be your own worst enemy; don't be too kind-hearted. You will get taken in by people who want to use you. In love, if you want to know if this is the person you should marry, the answer is, no.

VI
The Lovers

Meaning: Choice between two lovers. There are two messages in the cards. Lovers can mean two people loving each other, or a new romance is coming, or a new relationship can be just around the corner. You may have to make a choice between two people that you love equally. Tough decision. Choose wisely.

The Lovers Reversed

Parting of the ways, the end of a relationship. Whether this is temporary or permanent depends on all the other cards. If an abundance of Sword cards comes up, the relationship is temporary and the split is permanent.

VII
The Chariot

Meaning: The Chariot means traveling by car. You may be buying a new car. You may be traveling soon in connection with work. If The Lovers show up near The Chariot, it means riding in a car with a loved one.

The Chariot Reversed

Car Problems. If other cards such as swords appear, it might mean a car accident, beware.

VIII
Strength

Meaning: You have the strength to see things through. This card shows that somebody who has been ill is going to recover soon. You will be able to overcome future problems and have the courage to cope with all matters; you will triumph over people who are jealous over you.

Strength Reversed

Continued health problems, or someone drained of energy; there is a possibility that the struggle will be too much for them. Learn to let go.

IX
The Hermit

Meaning: One who is in a hermit cell, who has backed away from the world. He doesn't want to be bothered, there could be an important decision he needs to make. Let him think things through alone.

The Hermit Reversed

One who has backed away from the world. The key here is a failure to grow up and see things the way they are. Child-like tendencies; he is afraid to move in any direction. If the questioner is asking, "Will someone come back into my life?," the answer is, no.

X
Wheel of
Fortune

Meaning: Round the Wheel goes, where she stops, no one knows; the Wheel spins you a treasure. The Wheel signifies change with ups and downs, highs and lows; you are being told that nothing stays forever. The Wheel's ever-changing indicates a change for the better, a change coming out of the blue, a stroke of luck, great opportunity, or even a God-send.

Wheel of Fortune Reversed

Unexpected set back. This may be the end of a trying time. The beginning of some new things to come; however, there are delays in receiving money or property.

XI
Justice

Meaning: Justice, fair play, and balance. This card often comes up when there are legal matters with which you must contend; on the whole, it can be good. It's a great card to have when you are about to go into partnership with someone new; or, if you are fighting a legal battle, you should come out on top.

Justice Reversed

Legal problems will not be resolved. The legal problems will continue. An unfair decision will come down.

XII
The Hanged
Man

Meaning: One who is suspended in air: he is hung up and can't make any decisions in work, business, or any given thing, at this time. It will take time to see things through. Try to help him make a sensible decision. If the hanged man is you, time is passing you by—wake up, make a decision, and stick to it. If this card is near The Lovers, he is hung up on love and will eventually come to his senses; it also shows he may be coming out of a relationship.

The Hanged Man Reversed

Someone who wants change but is unable to face any situation at this time. He is child-like in his thinking. Eventually he will come out of this, and this phase will come to an end.

XIII
Death

Meaning: Can mean physical death or a shock; good or bad, depending on other cards, a rapid change. If the Death card falls near the Ace of Swords, the Seven of Swords, the Eight of Swords, or the Nine of Swords, all in the same layout, someone will pass on in the family. Or you will hear of a death, of someone close to you. All these cards must be in the layout at once, to indicate death. If The Tower comes up, it is sure to come to pass. If none of the high cards appear, or The Tower, it indicates a shock, good or bad, depending on other cards.

Example: If the Death card comes near the Pentacles or money cards, it indicates a shock about getting money. This can be a good shock. The Death card is not always bad; it also means change and transformation—everything around you is going to change.

Death Reversed

Illness, not so dramatic. Lighter shock; when this card is in reverse, it just lessens the meaning of the card. Death delayed.

XIV
Temperance

Meaning: Moderation in all you do; moderation in life is what she is all about. Time to relax. Don't overdo at this time. Use moderation. Don't take on any new projects yet.

Temperance Reversed

Too busy to even think you will be on the go. One who is overdoing it. If he is not careful, he will end up quite sick. You are taking on too much responsibility. Use moderation in all you do.

THE DEVIL .

XV
The Devil

Meaning: Overindulgence in food, drink, sex, or alcohol. This is the card of compulsion—one who may drink, have too much sex, too much of anything—one who is addicted. He is bound by his indulgences; he must seek help and break the chains that bind him.

The Devil Reversed

The questioner is in for trouble. Be careful! Watch out! For the police, from overindulgences. He could spend time in jail.

XVI
The Tower

Meaning: Everything has fallen, there is nothing left. The Tower refers to any given question that you have asked the cards, such as, "How is my business doing"? The answer would be, a calamity, loss, everything is going to be destroyed. But sometimes this clears the way for new and exciting things in the future. It may be just what you need to start a new business, or it may turn out better, but the actual meaning is loss of everything near and dear, even bankruptcy.

The Tower Reversed

You are now seeing things clearly. Now you are able to learn from the mess; new beginnings are able to happen now; look for the sunshine after the rain.

XVII
The Star

Meaning: The Star of high hopes and aspirations. Things look optimistic at this time. Things will go well for you if it is applied to career. If in a love situation, things will go well; highest hopes for you now.

The Star Reversed

Warning not to expand horizons now. It is not the time. A delay in plans; things are not what they seem. Use caution in all you do, don't jump into any new ventures at this time.

XVIII
The Moon

Meaning: Things that go bump in the night. A time card; don't travel, don't begin new ventures; things are out of whack, like the full moon; let things go for now. If the questioner has fallen in love, and they are not sure how things are going, this card will appear, meaning the relationship is going nowhere. If they are dealing with money or work, there is trickery in the air; also in air travel—this is not a good time to travel. This is a time card. If The Sun card and The Moon card fall next to each other, it means things happen in the early morning.

Moon Reversed

This card just lessens the meaning of the card. Things are not what they seem. Caution in travel. Love takes a back seat.

XIX
The Sun

Meaning: Happiness is on its way. If you have asked a question that requires a yes or no answer, the answer is always, yes, especially when The Sun appears in the tenth position.

The Sun Reversed

Happiness is delayed; it doesn't mean you will not get your wish, it is just delayed.

XX
Judgment

Meaning: You are being judged; a phase is coming to its end; let it phase out. The Judgment card can mean that you will be getting just rewards, or, if in a legal matter, you will be judged fairly. There will be retirement parties, and also there may be a promotion in the future.

Judgment Reversed

Legal matters may not turn out the way you wanted.

XXI
The World

Meaning: Travel coming soon. There are many turning points that are coming up. There are good times ahead through travel and good fortune. You are about to feel inner peace. This may mean a move or travel to a distant place or a new state, a new beginning ahead in a new place.

The World Reversed

Inability to accept change. You want to stay in a rut; try traveling more.

31

THE MINOR ARCANA

<u>Wands</u>	Business and Enterprise
<u>Cups</u>	Love, Marriage, and Friendship
<u>Swords</u>	Sadness and Sorrow
<u>Pentacles</u>	Money and Wealth

Wands
Represent Business and Enterprise

   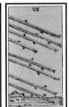

33

Ace of Wands An important telephone call that you will get; the start of something new; a job offer; a possible birth in the family; accept any invitation offered.

Reversed Don't believe everything you hear; it may be necessary to cancel some plans, as the time is not right.

Two of Wands Possible business partnership; it may mean a good property deal to come. Watch out for competition on the romance level. There may be a proud man who is, or shortly will be, involved with the questioner's life. Be on the lookout for an important letter or document; could be good news about property, or love.

Reversed Delays in the sale or purchase of property.

Three of Wands New business venture to come; starting of a new deal, a new job, or a new beginning. There could be travel in connection with work, or a phone call to start work.

Reversed Nothing good about starting business. Wait.

Four of Wands Marriage plans being sought out at this time; someone enjoying romance, laying foundations for marriage. Purchase of a house, or good holiday in the near future.

Reversed All of the above may be delayed; delay in marriage.

Five of Wands Struggle in matters of negotiation, but the struggle is worth it. There should be a good outcome. Watch out for verbal fights.

Reversed Let things go now; leave it alone, try another time. There may be legal problems ahead.

Six of Wands Victory, great news coming, legal battles won. Negotiations will succeed, agreements will be reached, and problems will be overcome.

Reversed If there is a battle upcoming, the other side will win.

Seven of Wands Struggle to maintain position, under pressure at work, or in some other situation. There is a constant battle now, but in time, problems can be overcome.

Reversed Too many obstacles; slow down.

Eight of Wands Arrows of love; travel is on the way in business, lots of new people to meet, friendship, and/or love to be found.

Reversed Canceled plans; jealousy; there could be a strike at work.

Nine of Wands Time to hold on to what you have, as there will not be too much opportunity to expand your life; there are too many people making demands. Stay put.

Reversed Loss of position or work. There is a chance you could lose your position at work; demotion; there may be illness on the way; be careful.

Ten of Wands Struggle with work; you could receive a promotion, but you must analyze it to see if it is worthwhile. Too much responsibility, or too much stress connected with work. Relax at this time.

Reversed Burdens can and will be put down shortly; but that promotion and extra responsibility will not be coming just yet.

Page of Wands An intelligent, restless youngster who has charm and plenty to say; there may also be visitors, young ones from a long distance. There may also be surprising news on the way.

Reversed There may be problems with young ones at this time. There may be a delay, or some sort of problem with regard to contracts or travel.

Knight of Wands Business or news having to do with travel; a visitor from afar; a house move may be in the offing. Changes are coming, and they will require phone calls, letters and journeys.

Reversed This has something to do with travel, or travelers may be disappointing. A promise may be broken.

Queen of Wands A charming and clever woman, a good companion and a good talker. This lady is great fun; she is a good business-woman, a reliable worker, but not all that successful; she needs a good, helpful man behind her to boost her confidence in herself before she can really succeed.

Reversed This lady means well, but unable to be a good friend; or she really is an unreliable and unfaithful type of person.

King of Wands An amusing, friendly man who is fond of the questioner, but not necessarily going to become heavily involved emotionally. This man is good company; he will cheer the questioner up and may be very helpful in the working place.

Reversed This man may be great fun, but do not take him too seriously or get heavily involved with him in ways that matter. He is full of promises, but not willing to deliver the goods just now.

Cups Represent
Love, Marriage, and Friendship

Ace of Cups Start of a love affair, the beginning of an affectionate loving, or friendly association for the questioner. It could mean a romance of a lifetime, or a friendship of a lifetime. It may also indicate a ring coming, or a wedding.

Reversed Could mean the loss of a love; someone who did love the questioner may be getting bored now.

Two of Cups Happy hints of future I do's; a partnership; could have to do with an upcoming romance; it could be a business friendship—you could end up getting more involved, or making a commitment to each other.

Reversed Temporary parting of the ways, or a complete split in the relationship; it's possible that the relationship you want will not get off the ground.

Three of Cups Party or gaiety, a toast, good news on the way; could be a pregnancy, a wedding, a birth in the family.

Reversed Too much sex, too much playing, could indicate a divorce upcoming; a split-up or break-up possible.

Four of Cups Not happy with anything life has to offer; couldn't care less as to what really happens; no motivation; it shows the questioner has advantages under his nose which he can't see, but wants something which he does not have; or does not know what he wants.

Reversed He finally makes up his mind what he wants, or decides to make the best of what he already has.

Five of Cups Marriage or relationship appears to be breaking up. This card shows loss and sadness; however, it is not a total loss—there is something left over and he can rebuild for the future. He is looking back with regret, or even some kind of mourning.

Reversed The sense of loss is passing; there will be good times again. Possibly a meeting with an old friend.

Six of Cups Meeting with an old friend. There is a possibility of a job change and a chance to relocate. It shows you are reaching back into the past to rebuild the future.

Reversed A planned family get together will be a disaster.

Seven of Cups Too many choices, confusion; too many roads to choose at this time. Coast along at this time and refrain from following any roads for now.

Reversed Indecision, will sort things out eventually.

Eight of Cups Loss and regret; one who is miserable and depressed, but there is light at the end of the tunnel; one who is walking away from love, even though it hurts. A need to search for deeper meanings in life.

Reversed Ending of a terrible situation is now in sight. There should be some joy and fun ahead.

Nine of Cups Your wish card; if you have wished for something, it surely will come true.

Reversed Delay in your wish at this time.

Ten of Cups Marriage card. Happiness and marriage or living together; everything is going well.

Reversed A split is possible.

Page of Cups A loving, gentle youngster, light-haired, fair coloring. Often the pages are not people, but situations. The Page of Cups indicates a time to think and study. Possibility of passing exams; it often shows up when one is thinking of going back to school.

Reversed This may indicate trouble to come for a young man in the family. More studying must be done for someone to pass their exams.

Knight of Cups A kindly, good-natured, young man; a man who has feelings of love and affection toward the questioner. The questioner's lover or husband may have to go on a journey.

Reversed Love could be fading; a lover could be unfaithful, or just not right for the questioner.

Queen of Cups This woman is very loving; she is a good friend to the questioner. She will do her best in any situation. Although she is a bit spoiled and materialistic, she is also maternal and home-loving.

Reversed This lady may be disappointed in love in the near future, or unable to give her affections freely. She has been hurt before; she is holding back rather than be hurt.

King of Cups Lover or husband; kindly, warm-hearted man who cares for the questioner. Could be a bit possessive, but would be successful and happy in love relationships.

Reversed Probably quite caring and well-meaning, but not that reliable. This could indicate to the questioner that he is losing interest in this relationship.

Swords
Represent Illness and Sorrow

Ace of Swords Operation, worried, depressed, or sad. This may indicate an operation, or a cut to the body. As all Aces, this card may indicate the beginning of a new cycle. It could mean a very passionate love affair; whatever is coming to the questioner will come to him/her like a bang.

Reversed A business deal will turn out to be disastrous. Don't react too strongly in any given situation.

Two of Swords Can't decide what to do; so many decisions are ahead; you can't make a move or see your way clear of a situation; unsure. No decision can be made at this time.

Reversed The end of a stalemate. Things are starting to move in a nice fashion. There is relief from a difficult situation.

Three of Swords Heartbroken, being stabbed in the back. Third-party interference; there is loss, or heartache, to be faced. This could be the end of a relationship or some other sad event. Upheaval in a family situation; perhaps someone in the family has had or will have a miscarriage or abortion.

Reversed The end of a heartbreak; you may attend a funeral.

Four of Swords Your sickbed, but thank God you are not dead. This is a convalescent time to renew energies. This is a card of recovery from illness. This card will come up when someone is in the hospital, or you may be visiting a doctor.

Reversed Illness is there; more treatment is needed.

Five of Swords One who gloats over his defeats; quarrels, even violence. Someone the questioner loves may soon be going away. This card can mean someone who may be ruling by force. Break up, or severing of ties, could indicate that someone has run away, or left abruptly.

Reversed Intrigue and deception; someone is lying to you; be careful, look around you.

Six of Swords Leaving, splitting, or a trip by water, or over water. The ending of a relationship, a gradual release from poverty, or a great deal of unhappiness; could indicate a move, or a journey may be the turning point for you.

Reversed Journeys, even holidays, will be delayed; there may be financial losses.

Seven of Swords One who is on the lam; the card of the drinker or alcoholic. This card may indicate a robbery or rip-off; con artist coming your way. It also means one who wants to run away from everything.

Reversed Legal advice coming. Be careful of thieves.

Eight of Swords Vision blocked, with fear inside, cannot move. You want to hide. Someone concerned is both hurt and confused. It looks like you don't want to see what is going on in your life.

Reversed Restrictions will soon lift, but depression and hard times must be coped with first.

Nine of Swords There is severe pain and sorrow in your life; there could be illness, tragedy or a major operation that you will hear of, or you will be told of someone in the hospital.

Reversed Good news coming; be patient, don't rush things; the person that may be in the hospital will get better and pull through.

Ten of Swords The feeling is, you wish you were dead. There is a loss, could be legal situation, job, or social position. Collapse of plans which is difficult to accept. Separation or travel by water when this card comes up. This also represents problems with plumbing or pipes, or water or flood damage—watch for this.

Reversed Suffering from the aftermath of a deep personal hurt. It will take time to get over this; don't worry, time will heal your wounds.

Page of Swords This is an active, sporty child, who is dark-haired. There will be good news about business, but keep your eyes open: possibly scandal is on the way. A contract may need to be signed in the near future.

Reversed This young person may have problems to face. There could be disappointments regarding work and business matters, especially those concerning contracts. There may be someone unpleasant who is spying on the questioner.

Knight of Swords A tough, brave, and very intelligent young man may help the questioner soon. The questioner may make hasty decisions or sudden changes in the near future.

Reversed This could indicate an aggressive, destructive, argumentative young man, or just an active and ambitious man who has difficulties. Arguments coming soon, and swift action should be taken shortly. There could be some medical or surgical treatment soon.

Queen of Swords A sharp, clever woman, can be widowed or divorced. She may be a teacher, doctor or lawyer. This lady commands respect; she might be a bit too cool and prickly to make a good loving companion.

Reversed This lady is sharp and unpleasant; she may be cold-hearted and possibly spiteful.

King of Swords This man is dark-haired and rather sharp-featured; this could well be a doctor, lawyer or professional man who is about to have some important influence on the questioner's life. There may be problems ahead which he may or may not help. He appears to lack a sense of humor. If you were faced with financial or medical problems, you would be glad to see this card turn up.

Reversed This is an aggressive man who is bent on stirring up trouble. He may be the lawyer who is representing the opposition in an impending law suit. If you meet up with him, keep walking.

Pentacles
Represent Money and Work

Ace of Pentacles Important letter or document that you will receive; the beginning of something new. Be on the lookout for an important document, or a letter containing good news; a contract is on its way. Being able to get an educational degree.

Reversed Delay in a contract.

Two of Pentacles One who is weighing and balancing all decisions. There may be a break-up of a partnership or of a home. Property may be divided legally.

Reversed You may receive discouraging news, but keep trying.

Three of Pentacles This is the work card, getting a job, learning a skill, doing something along this line; new work in store for you.

Reversed Expect a delay, if you have applied for a job.

Four of Pentacles One who is thrifty and holds on to everything. Financial security on its way; he hoards things.

Reversed Short-term hold on to all money.

Five of Pentacles Loss; this may be trouble with government officials, CIA, FBI, involvement with IRS; could mean legal situation involving settlements or loss.

Reversed Problems coming to pass; there is sunshine after the rain.

Six of Pentacles Giving to the poor; good things are happening; promotion; having enough to give to others. In a divorce case, don't give up too much.

Reversed Things are getting better financially.

Seven of Pentacles Fate, luck, or gamble card; good finances.

Reversed Too anxious over finances. Don't be frightened.

Eight of Pentacles Work card; studying or learning new things, new training, new job or promotion.

Reversed One who goes to school forever.

Nine of Pentacles Unexpected check that you may or may not expect; also, great success from personal achievement can bring travel in connection with business.

Reversed Some success is on the way. There may be a gift coming, or some sort of cash delay in receiving your check.

Ten of Pentacles Fame and riches. Beginning to feel secure, free from monetary concern.

Reversed Short delay in fame and riches.

Page of Pentacles A steady, business-like youngster. This card brings news about money and possibly travel; however, in this case it

51

would be for business rather than for pleasure. A youngster will have good news soon that will bring about travel.

Reversed The young person described above will have some problems with money. Also, business and money news will be poor for a while; large sums of money will be delayed.

Knight of Pentacles A young man coming with news about business, money etc. Even travel and business are possible now due to the restless nature of the Knight.

Reversed Problems with work; could be a warning not to travel on business just now.

Queen of Pentacles This lady is money-minded. She is well off, or just determined to be so. She commands respect because of her status and possessions. She is a skilled, honest businesswoman.

Reversed This lady will win if involved in a fight against the questioner, especially if money is involved. She is tough and materialistic. Best walk in a different direction.

King of Pentacles This man should have good business sense, but will be cautious rather than a gambler or experimenter. He should be close to his family. He carries much wealth with him.

Reversed A hard-headed business man who is not on the questioner's side; he may look steady, but actually turn out to be a loser.

PSYCHIC DAYLE SCHEAR

Dayle lectures throughout the United States on E.S.P. She has an on-going television talk show called "E.S.P. & You" on a Honolulu CBS affiliate which airs several times a year, and, in her spare time, she is a guest on numerous radio talk shows.

TELEVISION APPEARANCES

Hard Copy Magazine (National Telecast & Australia)

New Year TV Special (FUJI-TV Tokyo, Japan—National)

Hour Magazine CBS (National Telecast)

The Late Show FOX (National Telecast)

AM San Francisco KGO-ABC (Regular 1 Year)

2 At Noon KTVU (Oakland)

ESP & You One Hour Specials (KGMB-CBS, Hawaii, 7 Yrs)

Your Future One Hour Special (KGMB-CBS Hawaii)

Hawaiian Moving Company (KGMB-CBS Hawaii)

Anchorage Live (KIMO-ABC Alaska)

Good Morning Alaska (KIMO-ABC Alaska)

ESP & You One Hour Special (KIMO-ABC Alaska)

KHON News (NBC Hawaii)

KITV News (ABC Hawaii)

Mystical Healing (Cable 22, Hawaii)

Daytime Show (KOLO-ABC Reno)
KOLO News (ABC Reno)
KHBC (Hilo, Hawaii)
Numerous Telethons (Charities)

NIGHT CLUBS

Harrah's (Lake Tahoe & Reno, Nevada)
American Hawaii Cruise (Cruise Ship)
Holiday Inn (Waikiki, Hawaii)
23rd Step (Hawaii)

RADIO SHOWS

21st Century Radio (Syndicated Nationally);
KGO, K101, KEST, KALX (San Francisco):
KSSK (K59), KGU, KULA, KKUA, KIKI, KCCN, I-94, KISA, KMVI, KKON, KPUA, KAUI (Hawaii);
KOWL, KTHO, KPTL, KLKT, (Lake Tahoe & Reno):
KENI (Alaska); **WWDB** (Philadelphia);
WCBM (Baltimore)

ARTICLES/OTHERS

The Washington Times
Honolulu Advertiser
Honolulu Star Bulletin
Honolulu Magazine
Tahoe Tribune
Reno Gazette

ABOUT THE AUTHOR

Psychic Dayle Schear more fully realized her Psychic potential when she randomly picked up a deck of Tarot cards. She studied the cards for ten years and devoted many years to giving free readings and helping people. She learned, over a period of time, that most everything she told people had come true.

Inevitably, the world-famed Psychic, Peter Hurkos, discovered Dayle's talent. Following their encounter, she underwent six years of vigorous training with Peter until his death. Dayle is his "only living protégé."

Dayle specializes in Psychometry: the art of holding on to objects to see into the past, present, and future. Through these gifts she has been able to solve numerous murder cases, as well as find missing children. Her special gift is helping people on a one-to-one basis.

Dayle is also the author of *Dare to be Different!*, which describes the eventful, spiritual journey of a Psychic, and *The Psychic Within: True Psychic Stories* (Blue Dolphin, 1994). Another book, *What If?*, a spiritual journey into one's mind, is forthcoming.

To address the author, write to Dayle Schear, P.O. Box 172, Zephyr Cove, NV 89448, or call (702) 588-3337 for an appointment.

BOOKS AND TAPES
by PSYCHIC DAYLE SCHEAR

Dare to Be Different! (soft cover)	$16.00
The Psychic Within: True Psychic Stories	$14.95
Tarot for the Beginner: Learn to Read the Tarot Cards in One Hour or Less! (book)	$ 6.95
Tarot for the Beginner (video)	$19.95
Tarot for the Beginner (book & video)	$24.95
What If? (book, forthcoming)	

BEST-SELLING BOOKS
from BLUE DOLPHIN PUBLISHING

Mary's Message to the World, Annie Kirkwood	$12.95
Are You Really Too Sensitive?: How to Develop and Understand Your Sensitivity as the Strength It Is, Marcy Calhoun	$12.95
Beyond Boundaries: The Adventures of a Seer, Louise Hauck	$12.95
Prince Charming Lives! Finding the Love of Your Life, Phyllis Light	$12.95
Mission to Millboro, Marge Rieder	$13.00
Dolphin Divination Cards (boxed set of 108 cards), Nancy Clemens	$11.00

SubTotal _____

Tax (7.25% CA only) _____

Shipping $3 + $1 for each additional _____

TOTAL _____

Order directly from Blue Dolphin Publishing:
1 (800) 643-0765
Mastercard, Visa, or Personal Check
Orders are shipped bookrate within 48 hours
Or Mail to: Blue Dolphin Publishing,
P.O. Box 1920, Nevada City, CA 95959

☐ Please write to be placed on our mailing list